BE WELL!!!

RAY R. AYERS, PhD, PE

Body

Spirit

Mind

To order additional copies of this book, contact:
Xlibris
1-888-795-4274
www.Xlibris.com
Orders@Xlibris.com

Church-Based Health & Wellness Ministry

A Proposal

Ray Ayers

rayayers@comcast.net

In Gratitude

I want to thank God and Dr. Chuck Simmons for providing my Calling, and my wife, Carolyn, for her patience with my Passion.

THE ISSUE OF AGING IN OUR CHURCH

Following is an exciting ministry idea and resource: Its inspiration came from responding to growing needs at Memorial Drive United Methodist Church.

Our mature members are living longer and struggling with the dual challenges of illness and navigating modern healthcare. At the same time, many of our middle-aged and younger adults are suffering—visibly or secretly—from unhealthy lifestyles. Even the most faithful among us, it seemed, are not truly "well."

So, after prayerful and communal discernment, a WELLNESS MINISTRY has been envisioned *"to enhance the health and wholeness of individuals and groups of all ages through a program of practical and spiritual guidance, assistance and empowerment."*

The good news is today the MDUMC WELLNESS MINISTRY is in formation, led by a Parish Nurse and dedicated laity. The better news is Dr. Ray Ayers, a key architect of this innovative program, now wants to help you to envision a "Wellness Ministry" for UMC and other congregations.

A research engineer retired after a stellar career, Ray feels God has called him to share his newfound passion and expertise with others—and I hope you will take him up on the generous offer. If so, I am confident your church will be blessed and Christ's kingdom served.

-      The Reverend Dr. Charles B. (Chuck) Simmons

CHURCH-BASED H/W MINISTRY
Mission and Vision

Vision: Given the longer lifespans and challenges of navigating modern healthcare, our church desires to develop a WELLNESS MINISTRY on a similar scale to, say, typical youth or music departments.

Mission: to enhance the health and wholeness of individuals and groups of all ages and stages through a multi-faceted program of practical and spiritual guidance, assistance and empowerment.

In The Beginning

- I Received My "Calling"
- My Qualifications to speak and to develop a H/W Ministry Program on this subject come from discovering that I can:

  - use the same engineering Oil/Gas R&D processes I have developed over 50 years
  - find Best Practices from 'Experts' to apply at our church
  - Use 2 M's: 'Methodist' and 'Medical Doctor' if possible

- But three years before, God had a book placed on my desk at work which told me to "live <u>younger</u> and <u>stronger</u> for <u>longer</u> with <u>passion</u>".
- Now all I needed was a plan.

SO HOW DO I LIVE
YOUNGER & STRONGER & LONGER WITH PASSION?

IT'S A BALANCE

Nutrition

Exercise

Passion

Most of What We Think is Aging is Actually Decay

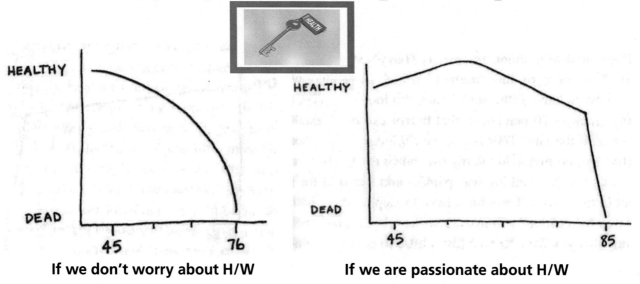

If we don't worry about H/W   If we are passionate about H/W

Our Big Finding from Memphis!

7 Segments to Keep in Balance for Healthy Living

(Proprietary Work of <u>www.ChurchHealth.org</u>)

The Healthy Living Model

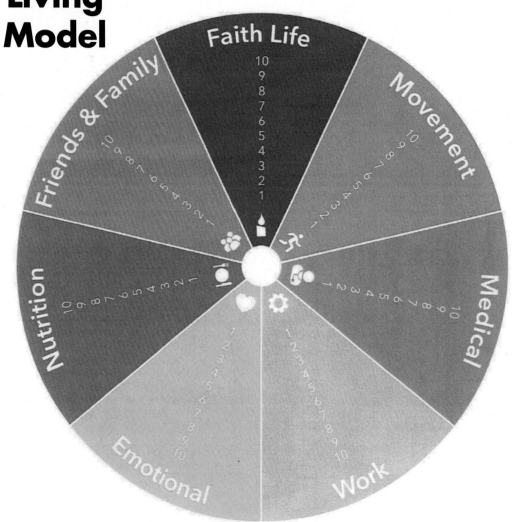

What Did Jesus say about Health & Wellness? See The Jesus Rx

by Rev. Leonard Sweet (20 years ago)

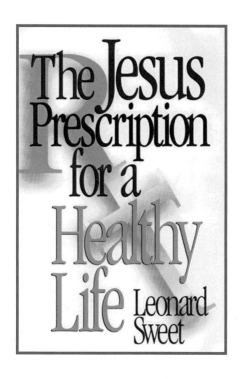

- Go to the Sermon on the Mount and find the Jesus Rx!!
- SPIRITUALITY is the missing 3rd leg to the Stool!!
- And SPIRITUALITY - in its Classic form - announces the presence of the Holy Spirit in each of our lives to keep us Healthy and Whole

For the Record:

Jesus and His Disciples:

- Had no motor vehicles,
- Had no McDonalds,
- But "Spirituality" was very close!

Elements of the Wheel

MODEL FOR HEALTHY LIVING	FAITH LIFE	FRIENDS & FAMILY	EMOTIONAL LIFE
	How does Sermon on Mount describe conditions for healthy living?	Include training for registry of persons in condfidentiality, etc. (Think Stephen's Ministry)	In Choir: Get Section Leaders who keep track of members and family issues. Contact missing members.

NUTRITION	WORK	MOVEMENT	MEDICAL CARE
Nutrition counseling	Priority: Set Workshps for Leadership Training: Communication with other groups		Include trainingfor registering persons in confidentiality, etc (think Stephen Ministry training)
Eliminate cookies on Sunday morning.	Pitch Volunteer Jobs we are trying to get people for aswork for God, using skills, talents, gifts he has given to us	Weight Room: women's movement	Volunteer Q+A Desk w/ library , resources
Have speakers come to educate us.		Adult sports teams, church leagues for volleyball, softball, basketball, badmitton	What about Screenings on Sundays (not Saturdays), whenpeople can come?
Lecture to us on Nutrition and offer different age groups, etc., more specific information.	Organize and teach groups.	Tai Chi Classes, Pilates, Yoga	Group registry of survivors of various illnesses available to mentor or counsel newly diagnosed.
Have church cooking staff put on Healthy cooking classes,		Offer classes for older, physically challenged people to move.	Same format for medical procedures - joint replacement, surgeries, involved medical testing.

Health & Wellness Ministry Framework

- You can use this "Frame" at your church to manage your H&W Ministry over the upcoming years.
- For each segment you can plan sermons, lectures, classes, and workshops to provide congregants information & experiences for growth. But you will need help!
- And The Medical Segment needs further definition, as shown next:

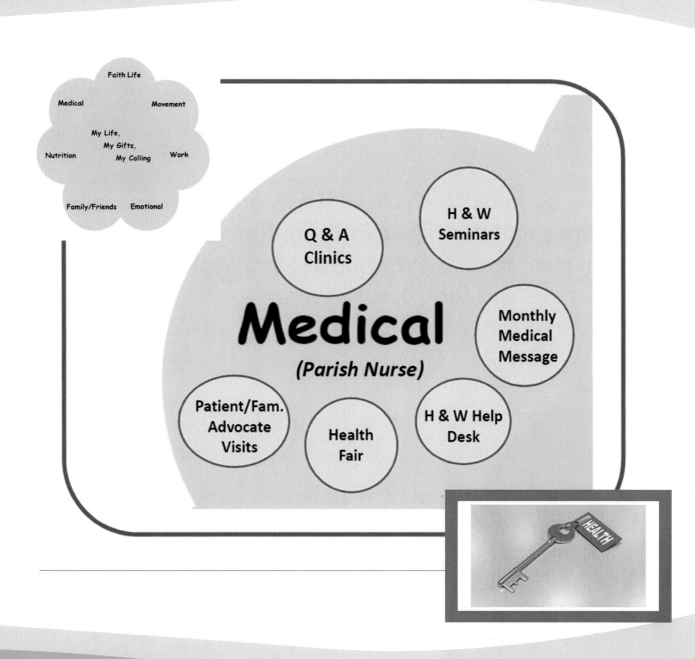

Faith Life

Medical   Movement

My Life,
My Gifts,
My Calling

Nutrition   Work

Family/Friends   Emotional

Q & A
Clinics

H & W
Seminars

Medical
(Parish Nurse)

Monthly
Medical
Message

Patient/Fam.
Advocate
Visits

Health
Fair

H & W Help
Desk

HEALTH

The Starting Point

- We are told: "We have all these 'groups' in our church - Let's empower these existing groups (like Sunday School Classes) to do H&W Ministry, and avoid overlapping".
- But we can form <u>Jesus Apprentice Groups</u> (JAG) for H/W Ministry Service.

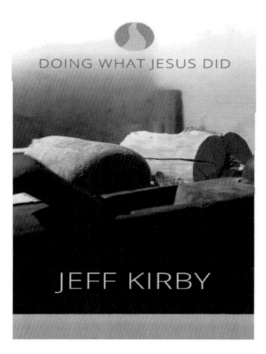

Jesus

DOING WHAT JESUS DID

JEFF KIRBY

The 3 Parts:
1. **Share The Good News**
2. **Heal the Sick and Suffering - HWM**
3. **Push Back Evil**

(Proprietary Work of Jeff Kirby at the Church of the Resurrection, www.cor.org)

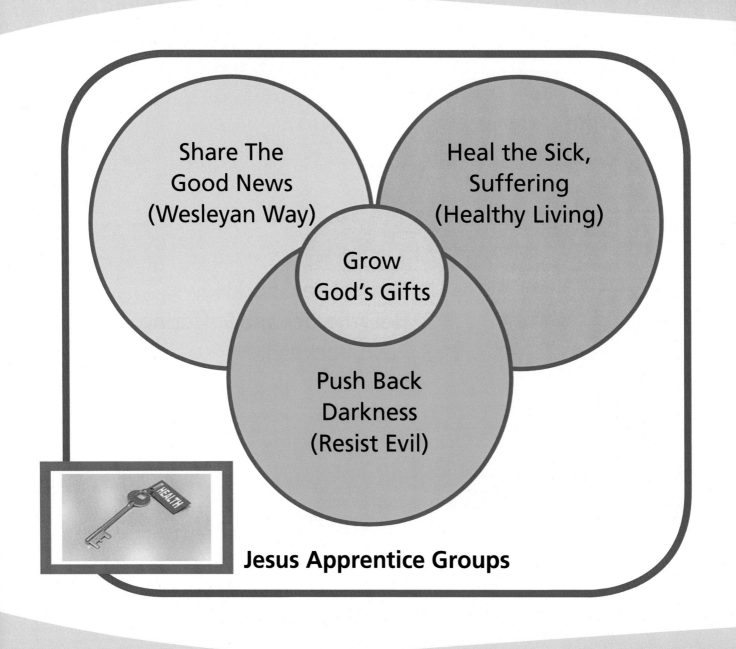

MINISTRY PLAN

A. **Use Scott Morris Book: <u>Health Care You Can Live With</u>.**

B. **Select opportunities to mention/encourage H/W in sermons.**

C. **Issue Monthly H/W E-Mails seeking communications on the <u>Model for Healthy Living</u> and encouraging congregants to find their "balance" in the Model.**

D. **Establish a H/W Response Management Process to deal with congregational issues with H/W.**

MINISTRY PLAN

E. Select one weekday as "Health & Wellness" Day at a suitable space for serving meals and conducting exercises.

- **10:30 am** <u>Balance and Movement</u> training (for older adults)
- **11:30 am** <u>Nutritious Lunch</u> (eating and education)
- **12:15 pm** <u>H/W Presentations</u> (about 30 minutes)

  - Medical Topic (monthly)
  - Nutrition (monthly)
  - Faith Life (occasional)
  - Family and Friends (occasional)
  - Emotional (monthly)
  - Movement (occasional, with weekly training as shown above)
  - Work (occasional)

- **1:00 pm Closing Prayer**
  Hold Medical 'Small Group' Meetings with Parish Nurse, with schedule TBA

MINISTRY PLAN

F. Schedule speakers on Nutrition monthly (with a focus on younger adult   members)

G. Organize Sunday Schools and other similar groups to offer their members to assist seniors and others who are disadvantaged in dealing with health issues while alone, like medical transportation, addressing safety issues in the home, etc. Issues discovered by D. above.

H. Set up Jesus Apprentice Groups (JAG) to assist in management and conduct of H/W programs.

I. Form a H/W Leadership Response Team to organize and conduct the above program, and assist the Parish Nurse, as advised by the Health and Wellness Council.

...when I said "nutrition", why did this show up??

H/W RESPONSE MGT. PROCESS

1. Congregant Makes H/W Request by:

- **Phone Help Line**

- **E-Mail Request**

- **Web Site**

- **Face-to Face**

Excel Workbook is designed & built to aid in managing the H/W process

2. H/W Helpline Team Member Receives/Documents Request &:

3. Confers with

- **Parish Nurse (medical) or**
- **Parish Minister (spiritual)**
- **H/W Team Lead (backup)**

as to Routing the Request to Proper Response Team

Yes: 5 (a) Route Request to Team Leader or Individual for handling

No: 5 (b) Route Request to Planning Team: (See Next Page)

4. Does Proper H/W Resource Exist?

HEALTH AND WELLNESS COUNCIL Advises the Process

H/W Response Resources

| 5(a) Existing H/W Caring Ministry Teams respond to Appropriate Request and Document the short-term outcome, and | **or** | 5 (b) Short Term: Parish Nurse and Minister attempt to meet the needs of the requester, even though formal H/W resources do not exist at MDUMC. |

| Initial Request and short-term outcome is documented in the Excel H/W Workbook | 6. Long Term: New Ministry Action Team confirms the need for a new H/W Offering and then designs and builds new H/W Ministry Offering, and, Information documented In Excel Workbook |

HEALTH AND WELLNESS COUNCIL Advises the Process

Parish Nurse/ Parish Minister Activities:

- **Individual Consults: Home and/or Hospital**
- **Group Consults**

H/W Response Resources:
Current:

- **Caring Ministries (existing) – See List**

Potential:

- **Adult Sunday School Class H/W Team Volunteers**
- **Youth Program Volunteers**
- **Men of Action Volunteers**
- **Boy Scout Troop Volunteers**
- **Volunteers at large from the congregation**

May the Lord Bless You and Keep You

Healthy and Well!

Printed in the United States
By Bookmasters